Plants and Tree Ecosystems!

From Wetlands to Forests Botany for Kids

Children's Botany Books

Left Brain Kids
Educational Books for Children

Plants and trees need places to grow and to multiply. Every creature on this planet needs a place to stay. Fish swim and live in the water. Birds fly in the blue skies and may live in the trees.

What is an environment? That earth has different environments in different areas. The environments vary in temperature, moisture and other factors.

Distinct life forms live in different habitats and environments. The living beings form complex communities of interdependent organisms.

Habitat is the place where plants and animals live. Plants and animals get what they need in their habitat. Their habitat supplies them with food, water and shelter.

Kids, in this lesson we will get to know some of the interesting ecosystems of plants and trees. Where do they live and how do they adjust to their environment?

Wetlands

Wetlands are known to be one of the most productive ecosystems in the world. They are where the land and water mingle. This area is filled with water. But some wetlands become dry in some parts of the year.

One of its functions is to provide habitat to wildlife and plants. The plants that grow on wetlands help control water erosion.

Deserts

These are very dry ecosystems. They can be in very hot or very cold parts of the world. A desert is place where there is very little rain. Can plants and animals thrive in such dry places?

There are plants that can survive with very little water. What are these plants? These include the cactus. Desert plants also have thick leaves to store in water.

Grasslands

These ecosystems are often flat areas of land. Grasslands are dry. They are hot in the summer and can be cold in the winter.

Grass is the main plant that thrives in grasslands, though there might be little bushes.

Forests

These are ecosystems in which many trees grow. Forests get enough rain and warm temperature for their bountiful trees.

When it is fall, leaves of many trees turn orange, red and yellow. Some trees lose their leaves in the autumn and grow new ones every spring. Other trees have green needles all year around.

Plants and trees are useful to us and the whole Earth. They help keep the environment balanced. Let us be plant and tree lovers!

There are other plant and tree ecosystems. Research and learn about them!

Made in the USA
Middletown, DE
17 January 2018